Colum Cille

Poet, Prophet and Sage

John Barber
Jim Killgore

Annals record that in the year 563 AD a boat landed on the south end of the small island of Iona. A group of Irish monks stepped onto the cobble beach and offered thanks to the Lord. Their leader was a man named Colum Cille. Over the next 34 years he would found and manage one of the most influential and powerful monasteries in these islands. To the people of Scotland he is better known as Saint Columba. 1400 years have passed since his death in the year 597 AD at the age of 75 and yet Columba's influence still endures. The 1997 exhibition, for which this text has been prepared, celebrates in objects, images and words the life and legacy of this central pillar of the early Celtic Christian Church.

Saint Columba's Bay on Iona. *Tradition holds that Saint Columba landed here and first established his island mission in 563 AD.*

SAINT IN AN AGE OF SAINTS

Medieval ruins at Gartan in County Donegal, Ireland. *Birthplace of Columba.*

Columba was born in 521 AD at a place now called Gartan, located in present-day County Donegal. His birth name was Cruimhinn which means 'fox' but he was baptised Colum, later rendered Colum Cille meaning 'Colum of the Church.' His family was part of the noble Ui Neill clan and could trace its bloodline to the legendary King Niall of the Nine Hostages.

Christianity was then a relatively recent introduction among the Celts and by no means universally accepted. Pagan worship was still widespread in Ireland, Scotland and Northern England. Yet by the end of the sixth century virtually all of the Celtic West and its fringe would be converted to Christianity by Columba and his contemporaries. This period was known

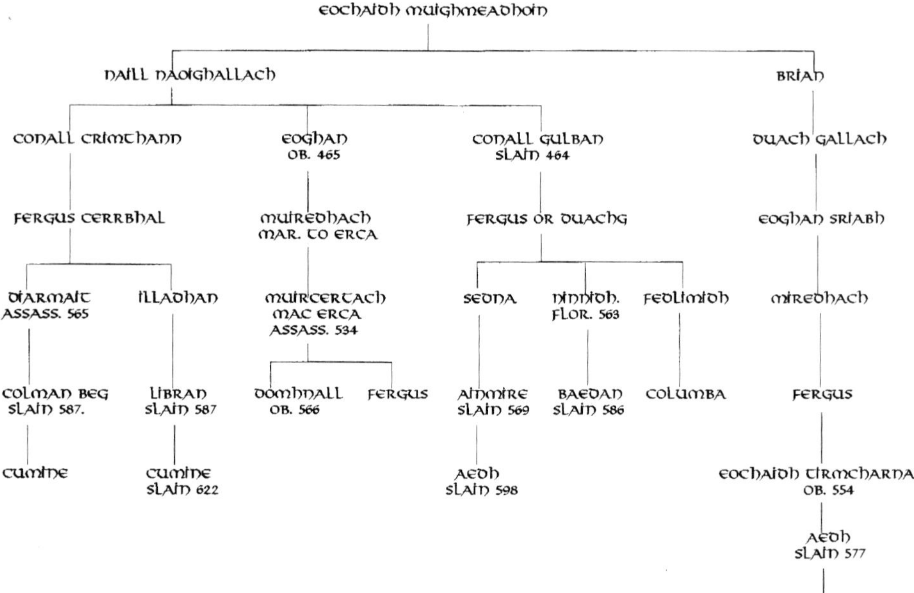

Family tree of the Northern Ui-Neill. *Columba was of aristocratic stock descended from the legendary King Niall of the Nine Hostages. Such standing leant political legitimacy to his mission.*

as the 'Age of Saints'. Columba was ideally suited to this mission, having an aristocratic Celtic background and a classical education within the church. This fusion of secular status and ecclesiastical learning provided him with the authority and skill to spread the Christian message in a manner acceptable to proud cultures, rich in their own traditions.

CELTIC SOCIETY

he pre-Christian Celtic West possessed a rich and complex culture. Society was rural, tribal, familial and hierarchical in its organisation. The smallest social unit of significance was the derbfine — the offspring of a common great-grandfather. The derbfine was responsible for the behaviour of its members. An individual's importance rested upon his position within his derbfine and its position within a larger tribe or 'kingship'. Exile from one's derbfine or family brought a kind of social 'death' and was known among early Celtic Christians as 'white martyrdom'; distinct from the 'red martyrdom' of being slain for Christ.

Boundaries between the kingships shifted almost constantly with shifting alliances. Often a tenuous unity existed among groupings of kings pledging fealty to an 'over king' or 'High King'. Dunadd in the Kilmartin valley was the seat of power for one such group, the Dál Riata of the West of Scotland.

An element of stability in this confused political landscape was provided by the learned classes or druids. The term 'druid' has been used to describe priests, poets, mathematicians, historians and legislators. Evidence suggests that such figures moved freely between kingdoms and were, in principle, respected by all.

Scholarship among the Celts placed emphasis primarily upon people rather than 'things' such as books. Julius Caesar records that a druid's training took up to twenty years, in which period all the history, laws and wisdom of his

Dunadd fort in the Kilmartin Valley - seat of power for the Dál Riata of the West of Scotland. *This view is through the entrance to the upper enclosure, with the citadel above.*

people were committed to memory. Writing was despised as a tool used only by those too stupid to remember. However, the Celts were not ignorant of writing. Ogham represents the earliest form of written Celtic in these islands. It is not a true Celtic alphabet but a codification of the Roman alphabet of the day. Surviving evidence of its use is restricted mainly to inscriptions on memorial stones.

Possibly the earliest surviving written Celtic language occurs on a calendar excavated from a temple site at Coligny. This object represents an attempt to reconcile the cycles of sun and moon — a common preoccupation of all early peoples and one that in Celtic society was the concern of the druidic priests.

The Celts seem to have had many gods, some

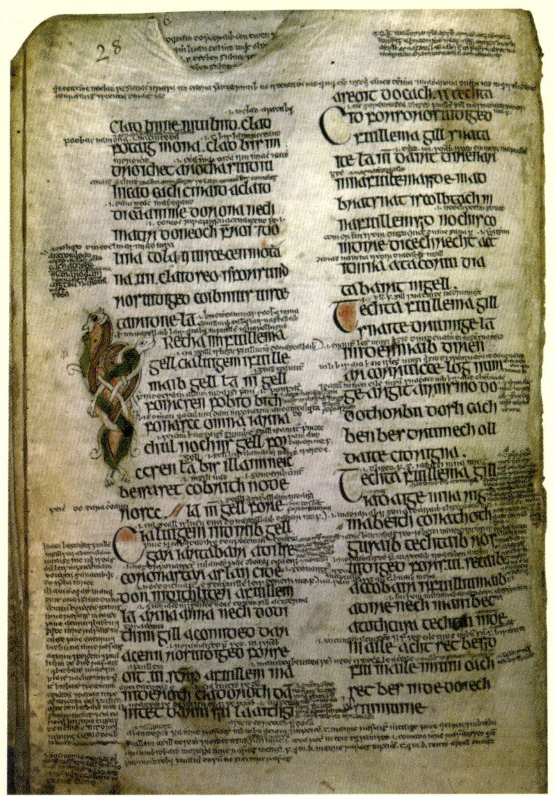

adopted from the classical world but others truly ancient. Aspects of the ancient sun god and the mother goddess can perhaps be dimly seen in later forms of Christian worship, the latter perhaps in the veneration of the Blessed Virgin.

Everyday life among most Celts was simple. Archaeological excavations of forts and settlements show that most larger households were self-sufficient in food production, the principal cereal crop being barley. Animals were also kept or hunted for meat and skins. Among the materials recovered from excavations are fragments of the bones of cattle, horse, deer, pig, sheep and seal, together with bones from a great variety of fish species.

Simple material goods such as tools and

Brehon law tract. *Pre-Christian Celtic society was unified in its observance of a sophisticated, although then unwritten, law code vested in a figure known as the Brehon who acted as an arbiter, umpire and expounder of the law rather than a judge in the modern sense.*

Celtic writing

Possibly the earliest Celtic writing can be found on a 'calendar' excavated from a temple site at Coligny in Northern France. The object represents an attempt to reconcile the cycles of the sun and moon -- a common preoccupation of all early peoples and one that in Celtic society was the concern of Druidic priests.

Fragments of the Coligny Calendar.

A later form of Celtic writing known as Ogham emerged probably in the Southwest of Ireland. It is not a true Celtic alphabet but a codification of the Roman alphabet of the day. Letters are represented by groups of up to five strokes cut across or along a central line. Inscriptions usually run up the left-hand side of a standing stone and are read from bottom to top.

Oghams are also occasionally found on small objects such as stone disks or spindle whorls. Most inscriptions simply record the name of a male and his father and, very occasionally, tribal and ritual associations.

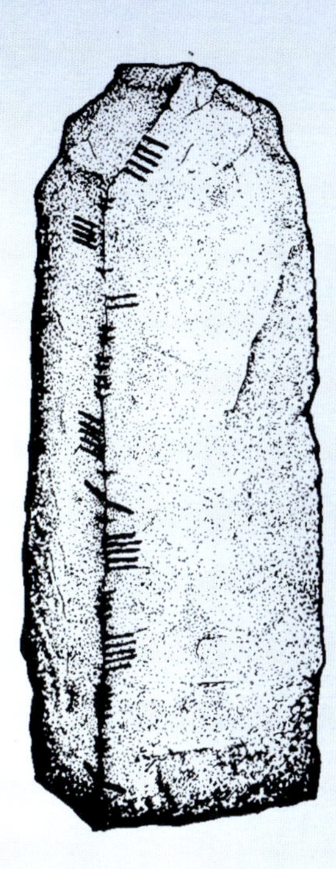

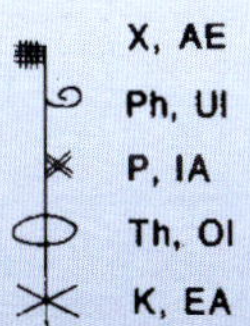

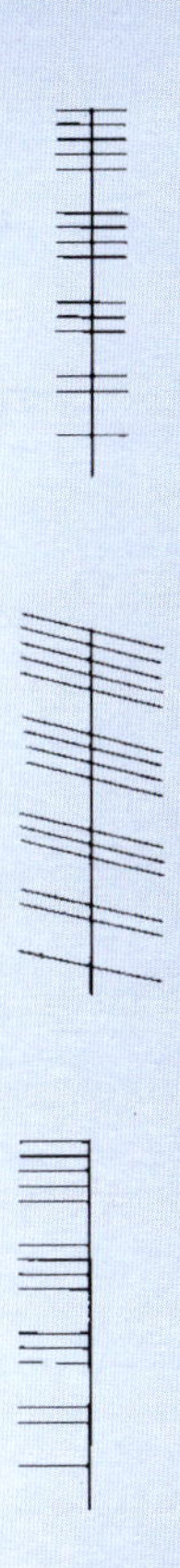

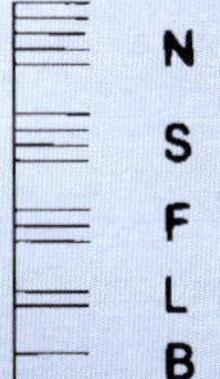

Main Ogham alphabet used in Scotland. *Letters are arranged in vowel and consonant clusters. On the stone to the left is a typical inscription which reads 'Moinena maqi Olacon' (Moinena son of Olacon).*

Aghascrebagh Ogham Stone. *Inscribed matter can be seen along the right-hand side of this stone from County Tyrone in Ireland.*

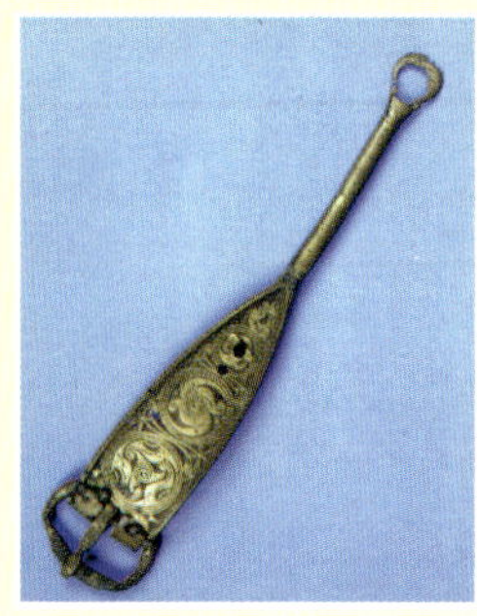

Decorated belt buckle found at Lagore Crannog in County Meath, Ireland (9th century AD).

Boa island heads (pre-Christian) at Lough Erne in Ireland.

clothing were also produced within the household. The Gaels of Scotland and Ireland rarely used ceramic vessels but relied upon wooden bowls and troughs, stave-built vessels and containers made from basketry and bark. Shoes and clothing were also home produced using leather tanned with oak bark and cloth woven from wool and flax.

Celtic glass beads.

Pagan female deity found at Caerwent in Wales.

Life among the more wealthy and powerful was not so plain. At sites such as Dunadd, master Celtic craftsmen wrought intricate and often brilliantly abstract works of decorative art in metal, glass, wood and stone. Such pieces pre-figure the exquisite work of later Christian masters.

MAN AND MYTH

'Ethne's Grave'
Traditionally held to be the burial place of Saint Columba's mother at Eileach an Naoimh monastery in the Garvellachs, Argyll.

Our knowledge of Saint Columba is derived mainly from the *Life of Columba,* written within a century of his death by Adomnán, ninth abbot of Iona. However, in this work and others, it is often difficult to distinguish between the man and the myth.

Foretellings

A number of myths surround the birth of Columba. Perhaps the best known is recorded in Adomnán's work but also in the earlier Life by Comine the Fair. An angel is said to have visited Columba's mother, Ethne, and presented her with an exquisite fabric which, in the vision, covered the whole of Scotland and the north of Ireland. This, he told her, was the area over which her son would one day spread the word of Christ.

Saint Patrick is also said to have foretold the coming of Saint Columba 100 years before his birth, at the baptism of Connell and Fergus MacNeill. Patrick rested his hand longer upon the head of Fergus and when Connell asked why, he replied that there would descend from Fergus one whose sanctity of life and hospitality would prove exceptional. This man's name would be Colum Cille. A priest called Moyty also prophesied the birth of Columba as did Movie Clairneagh with many others.

These tales can be read as biblical allusions. Ethne's story is similar to that of Mary and the visitation by the Angel Gabriel to announce her 'chosen' status as the mother of Christ. Saint Patrick and Moyty are characterised in much the same manner as Isaiah and other Old Testament prophets foretelling the coming of Christ. Stories like these are recorded in the 'Lives' or biographies of many early saints. Their purpose was to show that the saint lived a life modelled on that of Christ. This emphasised the importance of the saint but also, by association, the status of the writer as a 'keeper of the shrine'.

Education

Columba began his Christian training at a young age in fosterage to the priest Cruithnechan. Part of his education was also provided by a man named Gemmán who was later described as a Christian bard, suggesting that Columba received some elements of traditional Celtic learning. His later poetry, albeit written in Latin, supports this conclusion.

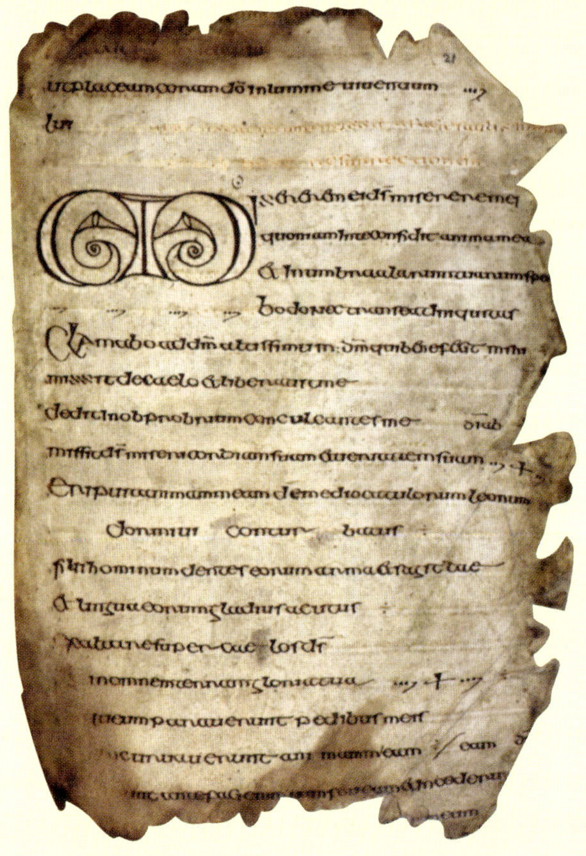

Manuscript page from the Cathac. *Probably the earliest written document surviving from these islands. This copy of the Psalter of Saint Jerome is traditionally identified as the book copied by Saint Columba without the consent of its owner, Saint Finnian of Moville.*

At his coming of age Columba pursued his studies under Saint Finnian, probably at Moville, and later he attended the monastery School of Clonard together with his cousin St Boyhinn. On the completion of his training, probably in the year 544 AD, he was ordained a priest by Bishop Etchen of Clonfad. He was 23 years old.

Early work and departure from Ireland

Columba founded monasteries throughout the northern part of Ireland. Among the most notable were Derry Columcille (545 AD),

Durrow and Kells (553 AD). But in about 560 AD Columba became embroiled in a conflict that would eventually lead to his exile from Ireland.

Adomnán is all but silent on the reasons for Saint Columba leaving Ireland. He refers to the saint's excommunication because of offences that were 'trivial and very pardonable' but insists that the decision was reversed. The nature of these 'trivial' offences will never be known with confidence. The indications are that Columba involved himself in political disputes between the southern and northern Ui Neill. Later legends describe his involvement in the battle of Cúl Dreimne, overcoming a magical druid's wall of fog or mist by the strength of his prayers. Later still, he was cast as the original cause of the conflict.

This version of events holds that the abbot Finnian of Moville brought back from pilgrimage a beautiful copy of a 'gallican' translation of the Psalter by St Jerome which he placed in his church. Over a number of nights Columba went to the church and made a velum copy of the book without seeking Finnian's permission. This copy is believed to be a manuscript known today as the 'Cathac'. When Finnian discovered the existence of the copy he demanded it as his own. Columba refused and both parties agreed to submit to the judgement of King Diarmaid. Diarmaid invoked Brehon

Ben Bulben.
Located in County Sligo in Ireland, this traditionally sacred hill overlooks the site of the bloody battle of Cúl Dreimne.

Gundestrup Cauldron.
Depiction of a battle scene in a detail from the Gundestrup Cauldron, Jutland, Denmark (1st-2nd century BC).

law and ruled 'as to each cow its calf and so to each book its copy'.

Columba returned the book but swore vengeance on Diarmaid. Tradition has it that he forged an alliance between the northern Ui Neill, the Ceneil Conaill and the King of Connacht in opposition to Diarmaid on the grounds of his 'unjust judgement' regarding the Cathac but also for allowing one Curnán to be slain while under protection of the church. A battle ensued at Cúl Dreimne in present-day County Sligo. Some 3000 are said to have perished in the fighting, a staggering number by the standards of the day.

Curragh.
Saint Columba is traditionally thought to have travelled to Iona in a curragh, a woven framed boat covered in stitched animal skins and made waterproof by oils and greases.

Diarmaid survived and is thought to have sometime later organised a synod of Irish Saints at the royal seat of Teilte (new Teltown in County Meath). Columba is said to have then been excommunicated by this body and, as a penance, exiled from Ireland in perpetuity. His confessor, St Laisrean, urged him to convert as many pagan souls as the number slain at Cúl Dreimne.

It is impossible to unravel fact from fiction in these tales. Certainly, the southern and northern branches of the Ui Neill were at loggerheads over the High Kingship of Ireland. Saint Columba involved himself in this struggle on his family's behalf. If he did not cause the battle of Cúl Dreimne he seems to have been involved in some capacity and this may have been sufficient to unite a faction of the church in Ireland against him. Excommunication on some pretext probably followed and, although subsequently set aside, it would have limited his 'career prospects' in Ireland. This and perhaps a genuine remorse for the harm arising from his involvement in the battle probably motivated a self-imposed exile.

Arrival in Scotland

Columba is generally thought to have arrived on Iona in the year 563 AD at the age of 42 years. Tradition holds that he travelled up the west coast of Scotland for a period of up to three years before that date. Other early texts suggest that he spent the two years following the Battle of Cúl Dreimne in Ireland, travelling more or less directly to Iona.

Conall, King of the Dál Riatic Scots, is said to have gifted the island of Iona to Columba. But other sources, including Bede, record that it was given to him by Bruide, King of the Picts. Iona lay on the Scotto-Pictish boundary and Columba probably petitioned both leaders to ensure a trouble-free settlement.

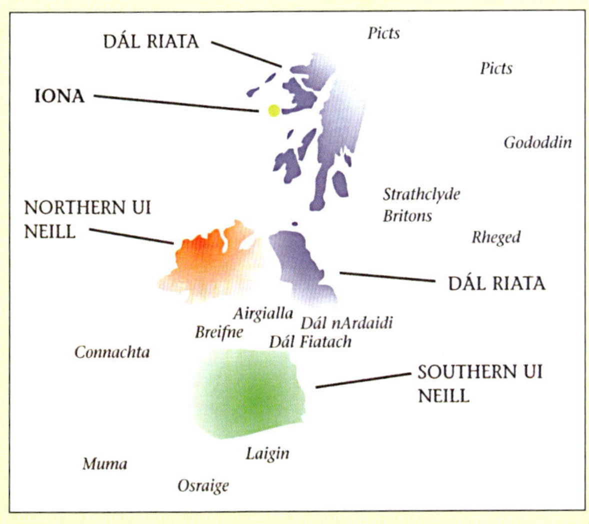

Major political groupings in Scotland and Northern Ireland at the time of Columba.

IONA

White strand of the Monks.
Site of the 986 AD massacre by Viking raiders of the Abbot of Iona and 15 monks.

he location of Iona on a standard map or sea chart gives the impression of a remote, isolated place, but at the time of Columba this would not have been the perception. An isochronic map demonstrates that in terms of sailing times Iona occupied a central position in the southern Inner Hebrides, accessible to the north coast of Ireland, the Outer Hebrides and the west coast of Scotland south of Lismore. In an age when overland travel was difficult and dangerous, the sea linked rather than divided peoples. Indeed, Iona was uniquely placed as a site for Saint Columba's work on the Atlantic seaboard of Ireland and Scotland.

Archaeological excavations show that Iona has a long history, and prehistory, of settlement. During the Iron Age in particular and leading up to the time of the Columban settlement, the island was inhabited and actively farmed.

The naming of the graveyard on Iona for Saint Odhran (i.e. Reilig Odhrain) leads some historians to speculate that there may have been an earlier monastery in place when Saint Columba arrived. Later traditions suggest that he 'evicted' two bishops, denouncing them as druids and burning their books. Perhaps these tales arise from a poorly preserved folk-memory of a pre-Columban monastery. In this context, it is interesting to note that the ditch of an early monastery on Iona cuts through an even earlier ditch of unknown date, a potential indication of an immediately pre-Columban settlement. No doubt the island's powerful sense of place would have appealed to early Christians equally as it has to later visitors. Even the inveterate cynic Samuel Johnson said of the island that he was a poor man indeed whose piety would not grow among the ruins of Iona.

EARLY CELTIC CHRISTIANITY

Croagh Patrick.
Penitential site of Saint Patrick in Ireland.

radition asserts that Saint Patrick introduced Christianity to Ireland in the fifth century and converted the entire populace. But historical evidence indicates that there were Christians in Ireland before Patrick and that many if not most of the population remained or had reverted to being pagan. Certainly by the time of Columba's birth, paganism was still widespread at all levels of society.

In Scotland Saint Ninnian introduced a form of Roman Christianity from his base at Whithorn in the Southwest. But his mission seems to have been no more successful than Patrick's in Ireland. Both men operated within a form of Christianity organised in dioceses, administered by bishops. Some monasteries probably had been founded but these were under the control of individual bishops and did not have the intellectual freedom of independent institutions. By the time of Columba's

Egyptian monastery of St Catherine's, Sinai. *The monastery, a religious community sharing a common rule, evolved from the desert hermitages of the Nile Valley.*

appearance the diocesan system had largely faded out of relevance, although traces of it could still be detected.

What the Columban mission brought new to Iona and Scotland was the monastery and monastic school: religious institutions dating back to fourth century Egypt and the monastery of Saint Pachomius. Monasticism was uniquely suited to the Celtic way of life. Early monasteries were self-sufficient ecclesiastical estates run by men dedicated to a life of prayer and learning. They produced their own food and material goods. Control was vested in an abbot who stood in respect of his monastery and its daughter houses in much the same manner as did a secular noble with his family and 'client' subjects. Monastic schools offered new intellectual possibilities: writing, classical learning, ecclesiastical patronage and new forms of artistic expression.

Christianity did not simply eradicate existing Celtic beliefs. Echoes of the older pagan culture persisted in some Christian practices and symbols. Pagan objects such as standing stones were probably Christianised, with Ogham or Latin inscriptions or carved crosses, rather than destroyed. Celtic druids worshipped in sacred oak groves known as Nemeton. Two of the earliest monasteries founded by Columba, Derry and Durrow, both feature the element 'Dar' or oak in their place names. It is probable that these places were already sacred to the local populace before being sited with Christian abbeys. Medieval accounts suggest that when Columba was gifted Derry by King Aed he sent his monks to cut wattles but they angered the keeper of the woods. Columba sent him barley which, although sown out of season, was nonetheless ripened and harvested in a miraculously short period of time. This probably

Nemeton.
This term refers to sacred oak groves used as sites of druidic worship. Some may have later been 'Christianised' as sites of churches and monasteries.

apocryphal story alludes both to Christianity's triumph over, and its incorporation of, established druidical practices.

A volcanic eruption in the year 536 AD is thought to have brought famine to Ireland and Britain over a period of ten to fifteen years. It was followed by an outbreak of plague (the Justinian plague) around 544 AD. Such a period of misery may have been enough to convince local rulers that the old gods no longer held any power, and this may in part have contributed to the success of Christianity. Adomnán relates that Columba on crossing the river Moyla in County Tyrone blessed it and forbade the plague to cross over the water. This seemed to prove efficacious. Perhaps the blessing with the aid of a little classical medical knowledge served to reinforce the new religion's power.

SCHOLAR

Columba's lasting influence can be measured in three key roles played out in both secular and spiritual contexts: scholar, statesman and patron of the arts.

Columba's claim to scholarship rests on his poetry, his skill as a computistical scholar and his work as copyist and writer.

Poetry

Columba was a poet of some accomplishment. The *Altus Prosator,* a poem and hymn, has been credited to his hand. It is an abecedarian poem: each stanza begins with a new letter of the alphabet — from A to B to C and so on. The rhyme scheme is complex and variable and the subject matter drawn largely from the scriptures. A shorter poem is also attributed to the saint, the *Adiutor Laborantium.* Columba's grasp of Latin metrical forms is indicative of Iona's involvement in the wider literature of the Latin church. His reputation as a poet of merit was established within his lifetime and was perhaps the reason why the poets of Ireland chose Columba to represent their case at the convention of Drum Ceatt in a dispute with the High King.

Manuscript page of the Altus Prosator - a poem and hymn composed by Saint Columba.

The Computus

Study of computus formed an integral part of traditional Christian education in the early Christian period. The term 'computus' refers to the ecclesiastical calendar, one of the main functions of which, for the Christian Church, was the calculation of the date of Easter. This relied on identification of the date of the vernal equinox and the date of the full moon that occurred on, or succeeding it. Easter was the most important Christian feast and, in turn, determined the dates of many other feasts in the annual Christian cycle. The determination of its date would later become the source of a bitter conflict between the Columban Church and the rest of Christendom.

A poem known as *Amhra Choluimb Chille* written by Dallan Forgill in the year of Columba's death provides some evidence of the saint's skill as a computus. The poet says of him:

> *'Seasons and calculations he set in motion...he put together the harmony of the course of the moon the course which it ran with the rayed sun, and the course of the sea. He could number the stars of heaven the one who could tell all the rest which we have heard from Colum Cille'.*

The date of Easter & ecclesiastical time

The date of Easter was a source of much controversy in the early Christian Church. It was the most important Christian feast and determined the date of many other feast days in the ecclesiastical calendar. Easter commemorates Christ's resurrection on the day following the Jewish feast of Passover. This starts on the evening of the full moon on the 14th day in the (lunar) month of Nisan, the first month of the Jewish year. By this reckoning, Easter fell on a different day of the week each year. At the Council of Nicaea in 325 AD, convoked by the Roman emperor Constantine I, the dating of Easter was changed so that it always fell on the Sunday following the first full moon after the Spring equinox. If this full moon should occur on a Sunday (and thereby coincide with Passover) Easter would be commemorated on the following Sunday.

Early methods for calculating the date of the feast proved unsatisfactory and Easter was celebrated on different dates in different parts of the world. In 387 AD, for example, the dates of Easter in France and Egypt were 35 days apart. About 465 AD, Pope Hilarius adopted a new method of calculation to reform the calendar and fix the date of Easter. Refusal of the Columban familia to adopt the proposed changes led to a bitter dispute with Rome in the 7th century.

Copyist and writer

Over 300 books are said to have been copied by the hand of Columba and while this is no doubt an exaggeration, there is a strong tradition identifying him as a copyist. The books were mainly texts of the New Testament and Psalms, probably for use in the many churches of the Columban Familia. Iona is said to have possessed a considerable library containing classical texts of contemporary ecclesiastical, computistical and philosophical works. It is clear from sources within the *Altus Prosator* and other works that Columba made regular use of this library.

Tools of the early Christian scribe

Manuscripts such as the Cathac or the beautifully illuminated Book of Kells were drafted on vellum derived from the fine skin of uterine or newly born calves. More heavily decorated folios required the thicker, more robust skin of older calves. It is estimated that the Book of Kells utilised the skin of 185 calves. To prepare vellum the raw skins were soaked in lime or urine and then stretched on a wooden frame. A semicircular 'luna' or knife was used to remove the remaining hair. Next the leaves were cut to size and ruled for text with wooden or bone tools. Monastic scribes used quill pens, often made from swan feathers, and iron-gall ink made with oakgalls and iron sulphate and gum arabic brought from Egypt. Pigment for illuminated manuscripts came from a variety of sources, including malachite, azurite, red lead and lapis lazuli. These were finely ground and mixed with egg or gum.

The preparation of vellum. *Detail from a 12th century manuscript illustrating the preparation of vellum. A square of calf hide stretched on a frame is being scraped using a luna knife.*

Chi Rho page from the Book of Kells. *The Book of Kells is perhaps the finest illuminated manuscript produced in the Dark Ages. Chi Rho are Greek letters commonly used as an abbreviation for Christ.*

STATESMAN

Iona as an ecclesiastical estate

olumba was no doubt an exceptional administrator. In the 36 years spent on Iona he oversaw the growth and management of a self-sufficient ecclesiastical estate housing a large community. Adomnán describes certain aspects of this estate that are still recognisable today. He identifies the 'machair' or little plain on the west of the island as the main pasture for the monastery. Cattle were milked in the field with the calves penned close by to ensure the flow of milk, which was then carried to the monastery in stave-built vessels. Adomnán also describes a mill for grinding corn. Recent excavations near the Coffee House on Iona have revealed a possible site for this mill. A nearby landscape feature known as Iomar an Tochaire probably served as a dam to flood the marshy Lochan Mor to provide both power for the mill in winter and a water meadow for spring grazing. Monks from Iona apparently had exclusive rights to cull seals on the rocky islands offshore from Iona, identified by one historian as the islet of Erraid. Shiploads of wattle from Mull and large pine and oak timbers from the northern mainland were collected for building. Metal and glass-working debris indicate that local craftsmen produced objects for use in the monastery but also perhaps as items of trade in the acquisition of off-island products such as new books or exotic inks or wine for mass. Columba as Abbot of Iona was responsible for the operation of all these activities.

Churches of the Familia Iona

Iona served as a base for the founding of new churches and abbeys throughout Scotland and Ireland. Administering to the needs of such a widely distributed community of churches must have required exceptional administrative skills even if they were largely self-sufficient units. Adomnán's *Life of Columba* indicates that Iona received many visitors, including representatives from other churches of the familia and beyond.

King maker, power broker

Columba greatly enhanced the prestige of his monastery on Iona by his involvement in the succession of the Scottish Dál Riata. In 574 AD the then high king of the Dál Riata, Conaill, died in Kintyre. His cousin, Eoghan, was the heir-apparent and, Cuimine (and Adomnán) insist, was favoured by Saint Columba. However, the Saint, who was on the island of Hinba at the time, was visited by an angel who instructed him to anoint Aidan as King. This proved an unpopular choice but the Saint managed to force his will upon the people. Aidan travelled to Iona and was there consecrated as King. By this action Columba demonstrated the Church's support for Aidan but perhaps more importantly its authority over the institution of kingship, in this the first Christian consecration of a king in Britain.

Iona's connection with royalty endured as a burial place for kings of the Scots, Picts, Angles and Norse. This practice continued into the Medieval period and later with burials of Lords of the Isles.

Negotiator and lawmaker

Adomnán's *Life of Columba,* like all the lives of Saints, draws many analogies with the life of Christ but also makes it perfectly clear that Columba was of aristocratic stock. Such standing, in addition to his reputation as a holy man, made Columba a respected arbitrator in the negotiation of agreements in secular Celtic society.

In about the year 575 AD Columba returned to Ireland to take part in the Convention of Drum Ceatt near Limavady in present-day County Derry. Here the newly crowned King of the Scottish Dál Riata, Aidan, met with King Aedh of the Irish Dál Riata. Columba was invited to help negotiate on three separate issues. First was the nature of the political relationship between the Scottish Dál Riata and the Irish King; second was the decision of Aedh to banish all the bards from Ireland because of their excesses; and third was Aedh's holding hostage of one Scanlán Mor for whose release Saint Columba had given guarantees. The convention eventually ruled that the Scoti (Irish) in Scotland were to go on 'hostings' or raids with the men of Ireland but were not required to pay tribute to them. Columba also won freedom for Scanlán Mor and negotiated a compromise between the bards and Aedh. Tradition holds that travelling to and from the convention the Saint wore a blindfold so as not to break his vow to never again look upon Ireland.

Dallan Forgill commented on Columba's legal prowess:

He was learning's pillar in every stronghold,
he was foremost at the book of complex Law.

Beccán mac Luigdech described him as

Columba, candle brightening legal theory

In the late eighth century many monasteries enacted 'laws' listing fines for various infractions which were to be paid to the monastery. One such law code is Cain Colum Cille or the Law of Colum Cille. The first article of the code recommends the foundation of monasteries close to principal centres of secular settlement. Although written two centuries after Columba's death, this law illustrated Iona's continuing determination to shadow and parallel secular society in the development of its family of churches. Among other statutes was one for the protection of women in time of war.

Cain Colum Cille. *This monastic law code was probably devised at Iona and incorporated a curious mixture of specific instructions and general advice. The copy shown here dates from the 8th century AD.*

PATRON OF THE ARTS

In the Annals of Clonmacnoise it is written:

Lastly St Columb said that hee had rather have his church full of Gould and Silver to found & build churches & houses of religion & to adorne the Relicks & shrines of Saints that they might be in the Greater Reverence with Posteritys.

Early Christian reliquaries. *A reliquary is a container used to house the relics of a saint, for example fragments of bone or personal equipment such as a staff or 'crozier'. Portable reliquaries such as these house-shaped shrines demonstrate Celtic metalwork at its finest, incorporating silver, gold and glass or enamel inlays and gem stones.*
Designs were often modelled on early Christian churches as in these two examples.

Medieval churchmen attributed to Columba the belief that beautiful craftsmanship wrought from the finest materials provided testament to the glory of God. Certainly Iona commissioned many precious objects to equip its churches and monasteries founded in his name. Among these were elaborate reliquaries of gold and silver, richly illuminated manuscripts, cross slabs and other church furniture. The Annals of Ulster record that around 553 AD Saint Columba placed the remains of Saint Patrick in a shrine, 'three score years after Patrick's death'. Even the small wooden churches of the period were said to have been works of art and so characteristic of the Scots (meaning Irish) that Bede, the historian of the Early English Church, described them as being built *modus Scottorum,* 'in the manner of the Scots'. Images of these churches can be found duplicated in portable reliquaries, as illuminations in manuscripts and other sources. Construction was of timber framing with shingled roofs and often a 'weather slating' of shingles on the external walls. As with similar Norse churches of later date it is probable that the walls were richly carved.

Celtic stone carving also evolved under the influence of the Columban church. At the time of Columba's mission to Iona the cross had begun to emerge as a prime Christian symbol and was often carved into simple stone slabs. This established a tradition that would culminate later in the ornate High Crosses for which the island is famous.

By introducing Christian iconography and traditions into Scotland and the north of Ireland, the church of Saint Columba created a need for new forms of expression in Celtic art. Patronage by the church fuelled a renaissance of work so beautiful that Geraldus Cambrensis (Gerald of Wales, 1146-1223 AD) could imagine them to be the works not of men but of angels.

8th century AD Irish crozier from Helgo, Sweden.

COLUMBA'S LEGACY

Adomnán records that Columba:

'...died on Whit Sunday eve, the 5th of the Ides of June in Iona in the 35th year of his pilgrimage in Scotland and banished hither and in the 77th year of his age as he was praying in the church with all his monks around him'.

Thus did his life's work pass into the hands of a succession of abbots at the monastery of Iona.

Columba's legacy lies not just in a reckoning of pagan souls converted to Christianity. It is in his method, in the manner in which he adapted Christianity within a Celtic context such that it could be embraced by that culture. In introducing monasticism, a form of religious practice organised along lines familiar to secular society, he rendered Christianity more acceptable to the Celts. Being himself an aristocrat of that culture, he respected the social institutions and learning of Celtic society and thus leant authority to his Christian mission. To the Celtic arts his church brought a new focus and vitality which would inspire a brilliant renaissance in decorative art and writing. Christianity opened up Scotland and Ireland to the wider world and brought increased trade and contact with mainland Europe. This was in no small part due to the influence of Saint Columba and ultimately to his own wisdom, dedication and love of God.

THE COLUMBAN INHERITANCE

Work of angels-Fine metalwork

A flowering of Christian Celtic art took place in the centuries after Columba's death with the Church as a principal patron. Chalices, crosses, candlesticks, belts and reliquaries of all shapes and sizes were produced in precious metals and richly decorated with glass studs or gold filigree. Secular patronage also increased in the period with finely crafted penannular brooches testifying to the skill of Celtic smiths.

Rinagan Crucifixion Plaque. *Pagan Celtic motifs are married with Christian iconography in this crucifixion plaque from Athlone made in the 8th century. Note the knotwork, spirals and the exaggerated head size of the Christ figure.*

Derrynaflan hoard. *Churches of the familia Iona were supplied with bells, books, chalices and other church equipment such as this chalice from 9th century AD County Tipperary in Ireland.*

Production of Celtic brooches

Metal for the main body of the brooch was melted in crucibles held in iron tongs. Craftsmen made wax carvings of the brooch which were pressed in soft clay. The clay was then fired, melting the wax and leaving a faithful mould of the designs. Fine detail was added as glass studs or gold backing plates decorated with filigree. Gold filigree work was built up from simple wire elements twisted and braided in various ways or from small balls of gold variously arranged.

Metal working tongs. *Found at Nendrum monastic site, Mahee Island, County Down, Ireland.*

The Tara Brooch.

Detail of the Tara Brooch.

Various types of metal working filigree.

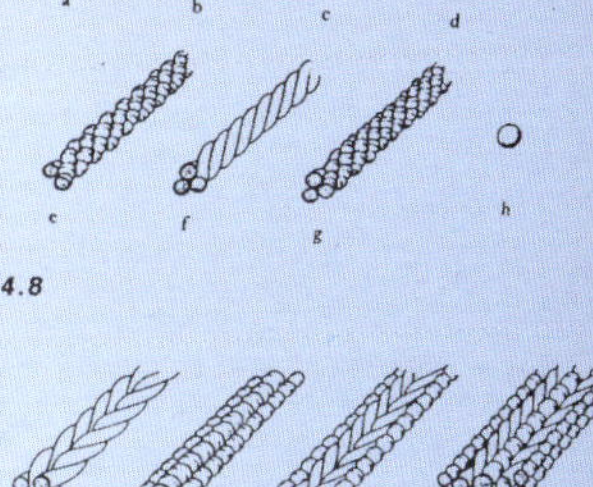

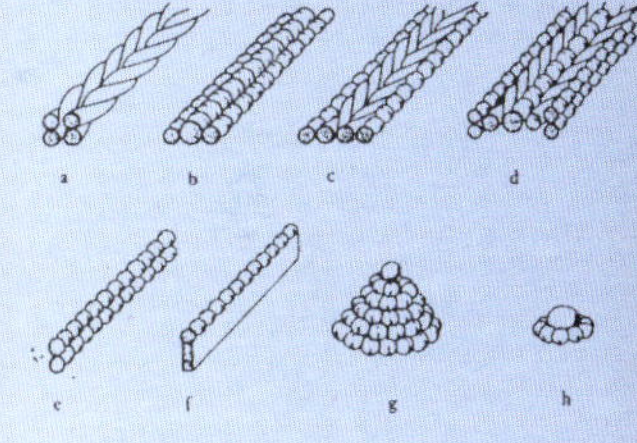

Detail of the Tara Brooch.

Work of Angels - Carving in Stone

The work of Celtic stone masons culminated in the intricate and imaginative carving found on the High Crosses of Iona. Here one finds older Celtic motifs interwoven with traditional Christian imagery such as the Virgin and Child. Crosses were used as burial markers or to set out preaching posts and areas of sanctity.

St Martin's Cross, Iona.

Replica of St John's Cross at Iona Abbey. *The original is in the Abbey Infirmary Museum.*

The Marian Cult

The status of women in Celtic society depended upon the class and family from which they originated, but in general it does not seem to have been high.The Abbey at Iona concerned itself with the status and fate of women from its inception. This is reflected in Adomnan's Law,

The Virgin and Child as depicted in the Book of Kells.

Cain Adomnán, which made provision for the welfare of women in times of war. Therefore, it is not surprising that the iconography of the Virgin and Child emerges through time in the works of the Columban church, from motifs incorporated on the High Crosses culminating in the famous image in the Book of Kells. This exquisite illuminated folio takes the form that was to become the traditional representation of Virgin and Child, but the 'child' is clearly represented with adult features. This stems perhaps from a reluctance to 'demean' the person of Christ by representing Him as anything less that a figure of power.

Panel from St Oran's High Cross on Iona depicting the Virgin and Child.

Book of Durrow carpet page.
This illuminated velum folio exhibits the free-flowing but highly disciplined virtuosity typical of traditional Celtic design. Produced in the late 8th century AD it is generally accepted as the earliest of the great Irish Gospel Books.

Lindisfarne Gospel carpet page.
The style of illuminating in this manuscript has evolved from that of the Book of Durrow, becoming more formal and rectilinear.

Book of Kells Eight Circled Cross page.
This manuscript may have been written and illuminated to mark the bicentenary of the death of Saint Columba. Note that the style of illumination is still quite formal yet there is a return to earlier Celtic motifs as seen in the Book of Durrow.

Work of Angels - Illuminating the Word

Libraries and scriptoria were the central focus of many monasteries. Copying of texts for use in the monastery or its daughter houses would have required the full time efforts of a significant number of monks. An evolutionary sequence can be discerned in the beautifully illuminated 'carpet pages' from the books of Durrow, Lindisfarne and Kells, all Columban churches. A more regimented and rectilinear format was gradually imposed on the free flowing virtuosity of earlier Celtic forms best exemplified in the book of Durrow. Marginal notes written by the copyists reveal a human side to the scribe's life. Hildebertus curses the mouse that steals his cheese, while an unknown Irish monk in eighth-century Corinthia pens a poem comparing his activities as a scribe to those of his cat.

I and Pangur Ban, my cat
'tis a like task we are at.
Hunting mice is his delight;
hunting words I sit all night.

Statesmanship

By the time of Columba's death Familia Iona had established itself firmly among the Irish, the Scots and the Picts. Later Columban missionaries would extend that range to the Britons in Strathclyde and the Angles at Lindisfarne. Eight of the first nine successors to Saint Columba as Abbot of Iona were members of his family, and this again mirrored organisation in secular society.

Perhaps it is notable that at the time of Columba's arrival on Iona the fortunes of Scottish Dál Riata were in decline but upon his death they were very much in ascendance. Part of the Columban inheritance was to establish the church as a principal player in the 'great game' of politics among the emerging nation

Dunadd.
Regional capital of the Scottish Dál Riata.

Tara.
The Royal inauguration site of the Irish.

Craig Patrick, Inverness.
The capital of Pictish Scotland is reputed to have been on or near this site. Saint Columba won tolerance if not outright acceptance of Christianity from the Pictish King Bruide.

states and in this we see the legacy of Columba's statesmanship.

Scholarship

In the centuries following Columba's death, the pre-eminent scholars in Europe were Gaels: Malsachanus, Dicuil, Clemens Scottus, Cruindmelus, Sedulus Scottus and Johannes Erugena. Study of the scriptures and other ecclesiastic writings required knowledge of Latin, and Latin grammar became the basis of all instruction within Celtic monasteries. Greek was taught in some early Irish monastery schools but was never a significant element in the education of monks.

At Iona a tradition of scholarship was established with the work of Saint Columba. The list of texts existing in the monastery library can be deduced in part from the poems and prose writing of later scholars at the monastery. These included some 21 named works as well as various concilar acts (or acts of church councils) and books of canon law, liturgical books and one or two Greek texts. A further eight to ten works are known to have been written on Iona. Perhaps most famous among these is Adomnán's *Life of Columba*. Adomnán also produced a number of other important texts including *De Locis Sanctis,* or 'Concerning the Holy Places' which forms the basis for and, indeed, the greater part of Bede's work of the same name.

By introducing the monastic form to Scotland Columba provided the basis for such erudition and opened the Celtic west to intellectual trends in Europe and beyond.

Cain Adomnán.
Adomnán was the ninth abbot of Iona (697-704 AD) and an outstanding scholar. In 697 AD he promulgated his Cain Adomnán, the earliest example of a law code composed by the Church but enforced both by Church and laity. This manuscript is probably a 9th century AD draft.

CULT OF SAINT COLUMBA

Saint Columba had not been long dead before becoming the focus of a cult of worship. An angel foretelling his birth, his raising of the dead and conversion of water into wine are incidents all described in the *Book of Lismore* and exalt his position to an almost Christ-like status. His relics were treasured throughout the Early Christian and medieval periods and became objects of pilgrimage. Even the texts he copied were invested with holy power and said to be able to survive immersion in water. The writer of the *Annals of Clonmacnoise* witnessed a book, possibly the Book of Durrow, being immersed 'unharmed' and the water then given to treat sick cattle.

Adomnán, like the biographers of other saints, might be said to have used such tales to 'manage' Columba's life story in order to enhance his image as a great saint and thus ensure the acceptance of his successors and the monastery. Some stories are also quite obviously intended to address issues more appropriate to the time of the writer than that of Columba. Adomnán's version of Columba's last words concerning the importance of concord and peace among his brothers was particularly apt in the writer's own day when the Easter controversy had created dissension within the Columban Church. In expressing Columba's great identification with and respect for the bishop Cronan, Adomnán again seems to address a contemporary issue: the rise of the powers of the bishop at the expense of the abbot. Adomnán's account of Columba's words to his attendant Diarmaid on the relationship

Monymusk reliquary. *A portable house-shaped shrine made to house holy relics of Saint Columba.*

between the Sabbath (Saturday) and the Lord's Day (Sunday) again address an issue controversial at the time of Adomnán but largely irrelevant to that of Columba.

By the medieval period, Columba had come to rank alongside Saint Patrick in the consciousness of the Celtic West and oaths were commonly sworn on both their names. The High Cross of Saint Patrick and Saint Columcille at Kells is dedicated in both their names. Later, when the Stone of Destiny was identified as the royal inauguration stone of the Scottish Kings, its credibility was enhanced by attributing it to Iona and Saint Columba.

Saint Columba's crozier*. A reliquary of a staff said to have belonged to the Saint.*

High Cross of Saint Patrick and Saint Columba located at Kells in County Meath, Ireland.

No evidence exists for a connection with the island and the creation of this myth illustrates the use of the Columban legend to validate persons, ideas and objects with which the man had no connection.

DECLINE OF THE COLUMBAN CHURCH

t the height of its influence the Columban church spanned five separate nations but even then the seeds of its decline had already been sown. Augustine played a significant role in the demise of the Celtic church in his role as 'Romaniser' of western churches. He arrived in Britain in 597 AD, the year of Columba's death, at the behest of Pope Gregory the Great. From an ecclesiastical centre in Canterbury Augustine sought to exercise his authority over the Celtic church, particularly in regard to the date of Easter. Resistance was strong, especially from the church in Wales. The English monk and author Bede saw this persistence as sinful, while, in contrast, Adomnán took the view that dissension and disagreement were greater sins than the wrongful setting of the date of Easter. Roman churchmen tended to dismiss the views of the Columban Church with no small degree of arrogance. Wilfred is quoted by Bede as commenting at the synod of Whitby:

'...I do not deny that they (St Columba and his followers) also were servants of God and beloved of Him, who loved Him with Rustic simplicity, but with pious intentions.'

The Easter controversy was brought to focus in Northumbria when in 664 AD the synod of Whitby ruled in favour of the Church of Rome on the Easter question. Later, around 710 AD, the Pictish King, Nechtan, in a move more political than spiritual, accepted the jurisdiction of the Roman Church and the

Roman versus Celtic tonsure

Tonsure is the term used to describe the ritual hair style of clerics. The Celtic tonsure was a remnant of Druidic times and involved shaving the head from ear to ear as seen on the 'Millifiori man' from the Book of Durrow.
A Roman tonsure involved shaving the crown of the head as seen in the depiction of Saint Columba in the St Gallen copy of Adomnán's Life of Columba.
By the time this drawing was made in the 9th century AD the Celtic tonsure would have been largely supplanted by the Roman style.

Celtic tonsure depicted on the 'Millifiori man' or the Evangelist Matthew from the Book of Durrow.

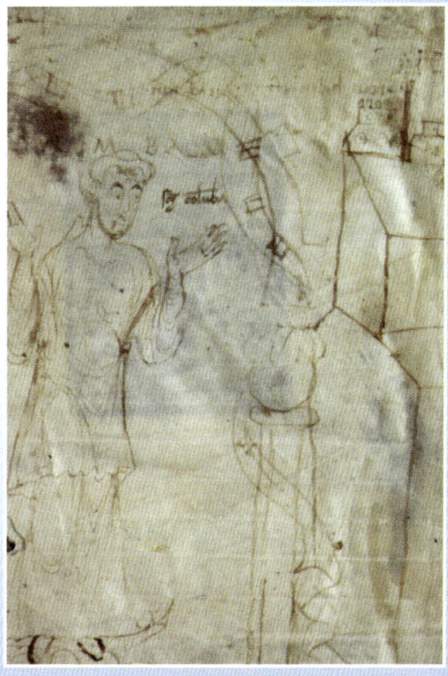

Saint Columba depicted with Roman tonsure in the 9th century AD Saint Gallen copy of Adomnán's 'Life of Columba'.

Familia Iona was expelled from Pictland. Armagh had meanwhile become a centre of the Cult of Saint Patrick and ultimately won the primacy of all Ireland, which it retains to this day.

Eventually the monks of the Celtic Church accepted the Roman dating of Easter and adopted the Roman tonsure, or ritual hair styling, but probably not until the year 716 AD on Iona and even later in Wales. The conflict led to the marginalisation of the Columban Church on Iona with power shifting to other ecclesiastical centres in Britain, notably Canterbury, and to Ireland.

Viking raids in the ninth century sealed the fate of the Columban Church on Iona. The island suffered one of the earliest recorded raids in 795 AD, a year that saw attacks also on Skye and on sites in Ireland. The island's position in the sea lanes of the Inner Hebrides, a boon in the days of Saint Columba, now became a curse under the onslaught of the Vikings. Defenceless against attack, the monastery became a place fit only for martyrs. In 807 AD the Abbot Cellach retreated to Kells in Ireland though a small community held out on Iona. Annals record that on Christmas Eve in the year 986 AD the abbot and fifteen monks were slaughtered in a brutal raid. One might assume this would bring about the final abandonment of the abbey. However, evidence from pollen analysis of a Columban period ditch suggests continual settlement even during the most difficult period, and the names of the abbots of Iona appear in the annals of Ulster up until the year 1099. Nevertheless, the raids certainly brought about an end to the Columban Church on Iona as a centre of power and influence.

AFTERTHOUGHT

Spirituality and the monastic form did not vanish forever from Iona. A Benedictine monastery was established in the 13th century and later a nunnery. These constitute the structures and ruins currently found on the island. In the year 1899 the Iona Cathedral Trust was established to care for these ruins and a programme of restoration was inaugurated which is still underway today. The 1930s saw the establishment of the Iona Community, who occupy the Abbey as tenants. Today many thousands of visitors sail to Iona to visit the historic buildings and ruins or to walk its more secluded paths, experiencing, if even in small measure, that powerful sense of place that first attracted Columba to the island some 1400 years ago.